M000303226

OXFORD BOOKWORMS LIBRARY
Crime & Mystery

Sherlock Holmes
More Short Stories

SIR ARTHUR CONAN DOYLE

Stage 2 (700 headwords)

Retold by Clare West
Illustrated by Guillem

Series Editor: Rachel Bladon
Founder Editors: Jennifer Bassett
and Tricia Hedge

OXFORD
UNIVERSITY PRESS

Great Clarendon Street, Oxford, OX2 6DP, United Kingdom

Oxford University Press is a department of the University of Oxford.
It furthers the University's objective of excellence in research, scholarship,
and education by publishing worldwide. Oxford is a registered trade
mark of Oxford University Press in the UK and in certain other countries

ISBN: 978 0 19 402420 4
A complete recording of this Bookworms edition
of *Sherlock Holmes: More Short Stories* is available.

Printed in China

Word count (main text): 8,351

For more information on the Oxford Bookworms Library,
visit www.oup.com/elt/gradedreaders

ACKNOWLEDGEMENTS

Illustrations by: Guillem/KJA Artists

Cover: Bridgeman Art Library Ltd (The Death of Sherlock Holmes, English School,
(20th century)/Private Collection/© Look and Learn).

The publisher would like to thank the following for their permission to reproduce photographs:
Alamy Stock Photo pp.56 (Law Courts, London/Classic Image), 67 (Arthur Conan Doyle/
Archive Pics); Getty Images p.66 (Ted Danson/CBS Photo Archive); Oxford Bookworms Covers
pp.69 (Sherlock Holmes Short Stories). (The Murder in the Rue Morgue; Rex Shutterstock
pp.66 (Joan Hickson/Moviestore Collection), 66 (Hercule Poirot/REX/Shutterstock).

CONTENTS

The Dead Coachman

The Last Mystery

The Dead Coachman

CHAPTER I

A Rest for Holmes

In the spring of 1887, my friend Sherlock Holmes was busy with a very big case. It was important not just in London, but all across Europe. He and I lived together in a house in Baker Street at that time, but he was away from home a lot while he was working on this case. He was often out of the country, too.

Holmes did not eat or sleep very much when he was investigating a crime, and I knew that he was working day and night on this one. So I was not surprised when he fell ill soon after the case ended. On April 14th, I got a telegram from the south of France. It said that Holmes was lying ill in bed in a hotel there. I left for France at once, and in twenty-four hours, I was sitting by his bedside.

'My dear Holmes!' I said. 'You look terrible!'

'Watson, you came. Thank you,' replied Holmes weakly. 'I'm not well, it's true. It has been a busy time. For the last two months, I've worked more than fifteen hours a day, sometimes with no sleep.'

'Holmes, that's bad for anybody, you know that very well!' I told him crossly.

'I could not rest while I was investigating this case,' he replied, shaking his head.

I looked at the many telegrams that lay open on the table. They all thanked him for his work.

'You caught one of the cleverest criminals in Europe, Holmes,' I said. 'He escaped from the police in three different countries, but not from you!'

'Yes, but I'm tired, Watson, I'm very tired.' Holmes lay back in bed and closed his eyes. His face was grey.

'Well, you must think of yourself now, Holmes,' I said. 'You need a good rest. I'm taking you home to Baker Street with me.'

'I'm tired, Watson, I'm very tired.'

Soon we were back in London. But Holmes was not getting better. He needed a holiday somewhere quiet, I decided. My friend Colonel Hayter had a large house in the countryside outside London, and he often asked me to visit. I knew that he wanted to meet Holmes, too. Some time in the countryside would be good for both of us, I thought. So I wrote to the colonel, and he kindly said that we could stay with him for a few days.

We arrived at the colonel's house a week later, and I soon felt pleased with my idea. The colonel was an interesting old soldier who knew many different places in the world, and he and Holmes enjoyed talking together.

The colonel had a large number of interesting guns, and after dinner on our first night, he took Holmes and me into his gun-room to show them to us. Just before we went upstairs to bed, the colonel said suddenly, 'I'll take one of these guns up to my bedroom, I think.'

'Oh, why?' I asked in surprise.

'Well, there was a burglary at a house near here – Mr Acton's – last Monday,' said the colonel, 'and the burglar escaped.'

Holmes looked up. 'Were there any clues?' he asked.

'None. But Mr Holmes, this little country crime won't be interesting for *you* after your great European case!'

Holmes smiled quickly. 'Tell me,' he went on, 'what happened at Mr Acton's?'

'Were there any clues?' Holmes asked.

'The burglar emptied lots of desks and cupboards, and left things everywhere,' said the colonel. 'But he only took two silver plates, an old book, and a small clock.'

'How strange!' I said.

'Well,' said Holmes, and he began to walk up and down, 'we can see at once—'

I held up my hand. 'You're here for a rest, Holmes. Don't start on a new case while you're still unwell.'

Holmes looked at me and stopped walking. I was pleased when we began to talk of other things.

But the next morning, the colonel's servant hurried into the breakfast room while we were eating.

'Have you heard the news from the Cunninghams' house, sir?' he cried.

'What? Another burglary?' asked the colonel.

'Murder, sir!' answered his servant.

The colonel's mouth fell open in surprise, and he put down his coffee cup. 'No! Who's died? Old Mr Cunningham, or his son Alec?'

'Neither, sir,' said the servant. 'It was William Kirwan, the coachman. Someone shot him, just once, sir, and he never moved again.'

'Who shot him?' asked the colonel.

'Have you heard the news from the Cunninghams' house, sir?'

'It was a burglar, sir. It happened last night, just before midnight. The Cunninghams think that this man was trying to break in, and William found him. The man shot William and escaped, sir.'

The servant left the room, and the colonel turned to Holmes and me. 'This is bad news,' he said. 'This will hit old Mr Cunningham badly. William has been his coachman for years. The murderer was the man who broke into Mr Acton's house last Monday, don't you think, Holmes?'

'The plate, book, and clock thief?' said Holmes, slowly. 'Perhaps. But it's a little strange. Burglars don't usually steal from two houses in the same village in the same month.'

'It's a man from the village, I'm sure,' said the colonel. 'Everyone knows that Mr Acton and Mr Cunningham have the largest houses here.'

'And are they also the richest men in the village?' asked Holmes.

'Well, they *were*, at one time. But there's a lawsuit between them: Mr Acton says that half of Mr Cunningham's land really belongs to *him*. So both of them have spent a lot of money on that in the last few years.'

'Well, if you're right and the murderer *is* a man from the village, the police will find him easily, I'm sure,' said Holmes, looking sleepy. He turned to me. 'Don't worry, Watson, I'll stay out of it.'

CHAPTER 2

Inspector Forrester Visits

We were still finishing our breakfast when the door opened again, and the servant brought in a young man in a dark suit.

'This is Inspector Forrester, sir,' said the servant.

'Good morning, Colonel,' said the inspector brightly. 'I'm sorry to come at breakfast-time, but I heard that Mr Holmes of Baker Street is here.'

'He *is* here, Inspector,' replied the colonel, and he looked at Holmes, who stood up and gave the inspector his hand.

'Mr Holmes, I'm pleased to meet you,' said the inspector. 'Could we perhaps ask you to come to the Cunninghams' house and have a look at this case, sir?'

Holmes turned to me. 'Sorry, Watson,' he said, with a little smile, 'this is not what you wanted.' He turned back to the inspector. 'Perhaps you could tell us what happened at the Cunninghams', Inspector.'

Holmes sat back in his chair to listen, the way he always sat when he was interested in something. I knew that I could do nothing now to stop him working on this case.

'Well, we had no clue in the Acton burglary,' said Inspector Forrester. 'But this time, both old Mr Cunningham and his son Mr Alec saw the man.'

'*Mr Holmes, I'm pleased to meet you,*' said the inspector.

'Ah!' said Holmes.

'It was quarter to twelve when they heard a noise outside. Old Mr Cunningham was in his bedroom, in bed, and Mr Alec was in *his* bedroom, reading a book. They both heard William Kirwan, the coachman, outside, and he was calling for help. So Mr Alec ran downstairs in his dressing-gown. The back door was open, and he could see William outside with another man. They were fighting, and the other man had a gun. There was a shot, William dropped to the ground, and the man ran across the garden and jumped over the hedge. Mr Alec stopped to try to help William, and so the murderer escaped. Old Mr Cunningham, who was looking out of his bedroom window, saw the man on the other side of the hedge, running down the road. But my men are looking, and they'll soon find him.'

'Why was William at the Cunninghams' house?' asked Holmes. 'Did he live there?'

'No, he lived with his mother in a small house on the Cunninghams' land. He's always been a good servant, so the Cunninghams think that perhaps he went to the

'The murderer escaped.'

big house because he wanted to know that everything was all right. People around here are afraid, you see, since the Acton burglary. The Cunninghams think that the man who murdered William was trying to break in through the back door when William found him.'

'Did William say anything before he died?' asked Holmes.

'Not a word.'

'Did he speak to his mother before he left their house?'

'She's very old and doesn't hear well, and we can't learn anything from her right now because this news has hit her so badly,' said the inspector. 'But we *have* found something important. Look at this!'

He took a small torn piece of paper from his notebook and showed it to us. There were a few words on the paper, and we could see 'at quarter to twelve' clearly at the top.

'William was holding this when he died,' he said. 'It's a piece from a larger page. And the time on it is the same as the time of William's death.

'I think that someone is asking for a meeting in this note,' the inspector went on. 'This is just an idea, but do you think that William was working *with* the murderer? Did they meet outside the back door and break the lock together? And then – we don't know why – they began fighting?'

Holmes was examining the paper carefully. 'This writing is very interesting,' he said. 'This mystery is deeper than I first thought.'

He was silent for a minute, and then said, 'Sorry, Inspector, you asked me a question. Was there a secret plan between the murderer and the coachman? It's possible – and a clever idea. But this writing shows...' He dropped his head into his hands, and stayed like that for some minutes, thinking deeply.

'*This writing is very interesting,*' Holmes said.

When he looked up, there was colour in his face, for the first time in weeks. His eyes were bright, and when he jumped to his feet, he looked full of life and just like the old Holmes.

'I'd like to have a little look into this case,' he said. 'It's a very interesting one. Watson, Colonel, can I leave you here for a short while? I want to go with the inspector to the Cunninghams' house to investigate one or two of my ideas. I'll be back in half an hour.'

But we saw nothing of Holmes for an hour and a half. At last, the inspector came to the colonel's house. 'Mr Holmes is outside,' he said. 'He wants all four of us to go to the Cunninghams' house together.'

'Why?' asked the colonel.

The inspector shook his head. He looked worried. 'I don't know, sir. Mr Holmes is very excited – strangely excited.'

'You needn't worry,' I said. 'When Holmes is excited like this, it's usually because his head is full of ideas.'

'Well, sir, he wants us to start at once, so let's go outside, if you and the colonel are ready.'

CHAPTER 3

Holmes Investigates

The colonel, the inspector, and I found Holmes outside, and while we walked to the Cunninghams' house, he talked about the case with us.

'I find it more and more interesting,' said Holmes. 'Watson, this visit to the countryside was a wonderful idea. I've had a very pleasant morning.'

'What did you do at the Cunninghams' house, Holmes?' asked the colonel.

'Well, the inspector and I examined William's body first. One gunshot killed him, that's clear. Then we spoke to Mr Cunningham and his son, Alec. They showed us how the murderer escaped over the garden hedge into the road. That was very interesting. We tried to ask William's mother some questions too, but she is very old and weak, and couldn't help us.

'The torn piece of paper in William's hand is very important,' Holmes went on. 'We agree about that, don't we, Inspector? It has the time of his death on it. I think that the man who wrote that note wanted William to come to the house at that hour. But where is the rest of the note?'

'I looked carefully for it, sir, all over the ground outside the back door,' said the inspector.

'Someone tried to take that note from William's hand,' Holmes said. 'Why did that person want the note? Because it showed who asked William to come to the house. It showed who murdered him. And what did that person do with the note? He put it quickly in his pocket. Perhaps he didn't know that a small piece of the note was still in William's hand. If we can find the rest of the note, I think that we will solve this mystery.'

'Yes, sir, but how can we look in the murderer's pockets when we don't know who the murderer is?' said Inspector Forrester.

'Well, well, we'll see,' said Holmes. 'Now here's another question: how did William get the note? Did someone take it to him?'

'I've asked at the post office,' replied the inspector. 'William got a letter in the afternoon post yesterday.'

'Well done, Inspector!' said Holmes, looking pleased. 'I am enjoying working with you, I must say. Now here we are at the Cunninghams' house. Come with me, Colonel, and I will show you the place of poor William's murder.'

We went to the back door of the house. Two policemen were standing outside.

'The fight between the two men happened here,' said Holmes. 'The ground is very hard, so there are no footprints. But Alec Cunningham saw it.'

Just then, the two Cunninghams came round the

corner of the house. The older man had a hard face with heavy-looking eyes. His son Alec had a bright smile and was wearing an expensive suit.

'Still investigating?' Alec said to Holmes. 'People say that you Londoners never get anything wrong. But you aren't very quick, are you?'

'Ah, you must give us a little time,' Holmes replied, smiling.

'You'll need it,' said Alec. 'I don't think that there are any clues.'

'There's one,' answered the inspector. 'We were just saying, if we can find—'

But the inspector did not finish what he was saying, because Holmes suddenly fell to the ground.

'Holmes!' I cried. His face was white, and I was very worried. We carried him into the kitchen and put him in a comfortable chair. After a few minutes, he began to feel better, and soon he got up slowly from his chair.

'I'm so sorry,' he said. 'I've been ill, and I'm still a little weak.'

'Shall I send you home in my coach?' asked old Mr Cunningham kindly.

'Thank you,' said Holmes, 'but it really isn't necessary. I'm well again now. And while I'm here, I'd like to be sure about one thing. Perhaps, when William arrived here, the murderer was already in the house.'

Holmes suddenly fell to the ground.

'Of course he wasn't,' said Mr Cunningham. 'Neither I nor Alec heard anyone in the house.'

'It is a mad idea, Mr Holmes,' said Alec angrily. 'Nothing has gone from the house. No one has touched a thing.'

'You must remember,' said Holmes, 'that this burglar is a strange man. Look what he stole from Mr Acton's – two silver plates, an old book, and a small clock!'

Old Mr Cunningham's face softened a little. 'Well, we want to help you as much as possible, Mr Holmes,' he said. 'Just tell us what to do.'

'First,' said Holmes, 'I'd like you to give a reward for anyone who can tell us about the murder. I have written this – please take a look and then write your name at the bottom.' He took a notebook from his pocket and gave it to old Mr Cunningham.

Mr Cunningham read the note. 'But you've made a mistake here,' he said. 'It says "at quarter to one", and the murder was at quarter to twelve!'

Alec laughed loudly, and I felt sorry for my friend Holmes. He was angry with himself, I could see. He never usually made mistakes like this, and I knew now that he was still not himself.

Mr Cunningham changed the hour on the paper, and gave it to Holmes, who put it carefully back in his pocket.

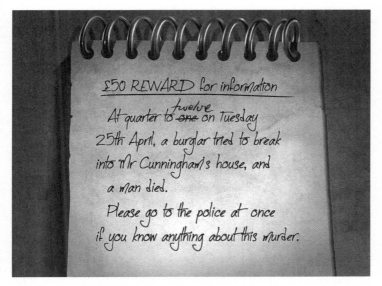

Mr Cunningham changed the hour on the paper.

'The reward is a very good idea, Mr Holmes,' Mr Cunningham said. 'Let's send this note around the village today.'

'And now,' said Holmes, 'I think that we need to look around the house. Perhaps the murderer *did* take something away with him – let's go and investigate. Could you take us upstairs, Mr Cunningham?'

CHAPTER 4

Holmes Finds a Clue

Mr Cunningham took us out of the kitchen and up the stairs to the first floor. He showed us the sitting-room, and some of the bedrooms. Holmes walked slowly behind him and examined everything very carefully. I knew that he was looking for something – I could see that in his face – but I had no idea what it was.

'Mr Holmes,' said Mr Cunningham a little crossly, when we came to the last two rooms in the house, 'do we really need to spend any more time up here? That is my bedroom over there, and my son's room is next to it. The murderer didn't go into those rooms, we know that.'

'I don't think that you're going to solve the crime like this,' said Alec, smiling unpleasantly.

'I would just like to look in your bedrooms,' said Holmes. He pushed open a door. 'This is your son's room, I think, Mr Cunningham? He was reading his book in here when he heard a noise – that's right, isn't it?' He walked in, and looked around the room.

'Have you seen everything now?' asked Mr Cunningham coldly, after a while.

'Thank you, yes. And now just your bedroom, if it's not too much trouble…'

Old Mr Cunningham looked angry, but he showed

us into his bedroom. Near the bed, there was a table with a plate of oranges and a glass of water on it. The others went into the room in front of Holmes and me, and when we walked in behind them, Holmes suddenly pushed the table to the floor with a big crash. The glass broke into a thousand pieces, and the oranges went everywhere.

'Oh Watson! Look what you've done!' Holmes cried, before I could say a word.

'Oh Watson! Look what you've done!' Holmes cried.

'I'm very sorry,' I said. I knew that I had to say this. I did not understand why, but I knew that Holmes wanted this to be *my* accident.

I got down onto the floor and began to look for oranges and pieces of glass. The others were putting the table back when suddenly the inspector said, 'Where's Mr Holmes gone?'

We looked round, but Holmes was not in the room.

'Wait here, all of you!' cried Alec. 'That man is mad! Come with me, Father, and let's find him!'

They both ran out of the room, and the colonel, the inspector, and I just stood there, in great surprise.

'I have to agree with Mr Alec,' the inspector began. 'Mr Holmes is saying and doing some very strange things—'

But before he could finish speaking, we heard a sudden scream: 'Help! Help! Murder!' It was Holmes! We ran into the next room, which was Alec's bedroom. Holmes was lying on the floor. Alec had both his hands around my friend's neck, and old Mr Cunningham was trying to take something from his hand. Quickly, we pulled the Cunninghams away, and Holmes got weakly to his feet, his face white.

'Arrest these men, Inspector!' he cried.

'What for, sir?' asked the inspector.

'They murdered their coachman, William Kirwan.'

The inspector looked at us all in surprise. 'But Mr Holmes,' he said, 'you don't mean that, do you?'

'Help! Help! Murder!'

'Look at their faces, man!' cried Holmes.

We all looked at the Cunninghams. The older man kept his head down. But his son looked angrily at us, and his dark eyes were like those of a wild animal.

The inspector went to the window and called down to his men. Then he turned to old Mr Cunningham.

'I'm sorry, sir, but I must arrest you,' he said.

At that second, Alec moved his arm up, and we saw a gun in his hand. But the inspector saw it first.

'Drop it!' he cried. He hit Alec's arm, and the gun dropped to the floor.

Holmes put his foot quietly on the gun. 'Keep that,' he said to the inspector. 'They used it to kill William, I'm sure. But *this* is what we really wanted.' He held up a piece of paper.

'The rest of the note!' cried the inspector.

'Yes,' said Holmes.

'And where was it?' the inspector asked.

'I'll explain everything to you very soon,' said Holmes. 'Colonel, why don't you and Watson go back to your house now? The inspector and I must speak with Mr Cunningham and his son, but I'll be with you by lunchtime.'

CHAPTER 5

Answers

It was about one o'clock when Holmes arrived at the colonel's house. He came into the sitting-room with a small grey-haired man.

'Watson, this is Mr Acton,' Holmes said, and I shook the man's hand. 'The first burglary was at Mr Acton's house, you remember. I asked him to be here while I explain this little case because it will be interesting to him too, I think.'

'Do take a seat, Mr Acton,' said the colonel. 'But Holmes, are you feeling better now? The Cunninghams nearly killed you! And before that, your fall – we were worried about you.'

Holmes laughed. 'I'll explain about that in a minute,' he said. 'But first, I'll tell you why that piece of paper in William's hand was so important in this crime. From the beginning, I knew that it was the key to the mystery. I wanted to know who tried to take it from poor William. Alec said that the murderer shot William and then ran away at once. So, if that was true, the murderer did not take the paper from William's hand. I knew that when old Mr Cunningham came downstairs, some of his servants were there already – so *he* didn't take it. Alec took it, I thought to myself.'

'Ah!' said the colonel.

'And then I examined the torn piece of paper. I knew at once that *two* people wrote this note together.'

Holmes put the first torn piece of the note on the table, and we all looked at it carefully while he went on: 'One person's handwriting is stronger – you can see his strong *t* in *at* and *to*. I think that *learn* and *perhaps* are in his handwriting, too. He wrote his words first, but he didn't leave much room for the person with the weaker handwriting. That person then wrote in *his* words – *quarter*, *twelve*, and *what*.'

'It's as clear as day!' cried the colonel. 'But why did two men write the note in this way?'

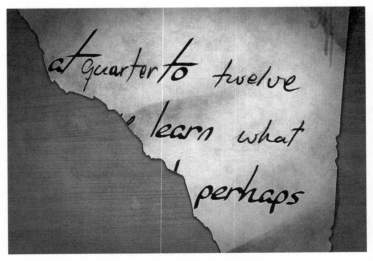

'One person's handwriting is stronger.'

'They were planning a crime, and one of them – the one with the stronger handwriting, I think – had the idea. If anything went wrong, he did not want people to think that he was working alone.'

'Very good!' cried Mr Acton.

'Now this is even more interesting,' Holmes went on. 'The one handwriting is very like the other in many ways. I looked at many things here, and I was soon sure of this: these two writers come from the same family. Young men usually have strong handwriting, and older men have weaker writing. The Cunninghams, father and son, wrote this note.'

'Very good!' cried Mr Acton again.

'Next, I needed to examine the murder carefully,' said Holmes. 'First, I looked at William's body. The shot that killed him came from about four yards away – but do you remember Alec's story? The two men were fighting when the murderer shot William, he told the inspector. So that was clearly a lie. Then I looked at the hedge next to the road. The Cunninghams said that the murderer escaped over that hedge. But when I examined the ground below it, which was wet, there were no footprints. So that was another lie. No murderer came to the Cunninghams' house that night – I was sure of it.

'So what was this crime *for*, I asked myself? First, I tried to solve the mystery of the burglary at Mr Acton's. I knew about the lawsuit between you and the Cunninghams, Mr Acton. So I thought to myself, perhaps the Cunninghams broke into your house to look for papers. Perhaps there is a paper that is very important in this lawsuit.'

'You're right, Mr Holmes,' replied Mr Acton. 'There's one single paper which will win the lawsuit for me. Luckily, it's not in my house, but at my bank.'

'Ah!' said Holmes, smiling. 'And, of course, when the Cunninghams couldn't find the paper in your house, they took a few things, because they wanted their break-in to look like a burglary. But I still needed one thing – the rest of the note. Where was it? There was only one possible place, I thought. Where do you put something when you find it in the middle of the night? In the pocket of your dressing-gown! That's why I went to the house for a second time. The Cunninghams met us, you remember, outside the back door. I did not want them to know about the note, but the inspector started talking about it. So I suddenly fell to the ground ill, and that changed the conversation.'

'Holmes!' cried the colonel, laughing. 'We were all so worried about you! But you weren't really ill!'

'No, Colonel,' said Holmes, smiling. 'After that, I wanted old Mr Cunningham to write the word "twelve" for me. And when he did, it looked just like the "twelve" on William's piece of paper.'

'So it wasn't a mistake when you got the time wrong on the note about the reward!' I cried.

'I know that you were worried about me when you saw my "mistake", Watson,' Holmes said with a laugh. 'I'm sorry about that. We all went upstairs then, and I saw Alec's dressing-gown in his room. So when we went into his father's room, I pushed a table to the floor, and while everyone was busy with that, I hurried into Alec's bedroom. I found the paper in his dressing-gown pocket. But suddenly the Cunninghams ran in, jumped on me, and tried to take the paper from me. I knew too much, and they wanted to kill me, I can tell you.

'After their arrest, Alec was wild and angry, but old Mr Cunningham told us everything,' Holmes went on. 'I heard from him that William saw the Cunninghams on their way to Mr Acton's. He knew that they were "the burglars", and he decided to make some money for himself. He told the Cunninghams to pay him a lot of money, or he would tell the police. But Alec was a dangerous enemy. He decided to kill William, so he made a plan, and he and his father wrote the note. They sent it to William, who came to the house last night. He was outside the back door when Alec shot him from four yards away. Alec pulled the note out of William's hand and put it quickly in his dressing-gown pocket. It was a very clever plan, but Alec didn't know that a small piece of the note was still in William's hand.'

'Alec shot William from four yards away.'

'Can we see the rest of the note?' I asked.

'Here it is,' said Holmes. He put the two pieces of paper in front of us. 'Look at the *p*s and *g*s – the two writers are clearly father and son. And old Mr Cunningham's *t*s are the *t*s of an older man.'

'Ah yes!' said the colonel excitedly. 'I can see it now. Holmes, you are a genius!'

My friend smiled. 'Well, Watson,' he said, 'I have greatly enjoyed our quiet rest in the countryside. Tomorrow we can go back to Baker Street, ready for work again.'

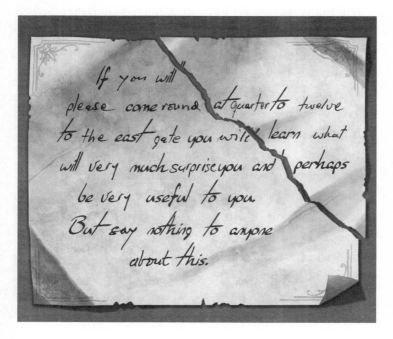

The Last Mystery

CHAPTER I

A Visit from Holmes

For a long time, I did not want to tell this story, but after two years, I must now write about what happened between Professor Moriarty and Mr Sherlock Holmes. I do it with a heavy heart.

For many years, Holmes and I lived in Baker Street together, but when I married, I moved away to live with my wife. Holmes still came to see me sometimes, when he wanted a friend to help him with a case. But I was busy with my work as a doctor, and I did not see him as often as before.

In the spring of 1891, Holmes sent me two short letters, and I also read about him in the newspapers. I knew that he was investigating a case in the south of France. So it was a great surprise when he arrived at my house in London on the evening of April 24th.

'Good evening, Watson,' he said, coming into my sitting-room. 'Could I close your shutters?'

My table light was the only light that was on, and the room was dark. Holmes went carefully around the room, closing the shutters, and all the time he stayed in

Holmes went carefully around the room, closing the shutters.

the dark, near the walls. Then he turned back to me.

'You are afraid of something?' I asked.

'Yes, I am afraid of guns.'

'My dear Holmes, what do you mean?' I asked.

'I am someone who is not often afraid of things. You know that, Watson. But when danger is near, it is mad not to see it.' He showed me his hand: there was blood all over it. 'It is a real danger, you see, not just one of my little ideas,' he said, smiling. 'Now, is your wife at home?'

'She is away on a visit to her family.'

'Ah! You are alone – that's good. Then can I ask you to come away with me for a week?'

'Where?' I asked.

'Oh, anywhere. It really doesn't matter.'

There was something very strange in all this. Holmes did not usually take holidays, and his face looked grey and tired. He saw the question in my eyes, so he sat down and began to explain.

Holmes sat down and began to explain.

'Have you ever heard of Professor Moriarty?' he said.
'Never.'

'That is because he's a genius!' he cried. 'The man's
crimes are everywhere, and no one has heard of him. He
is the greatest criminal in the world. I tell you, Watson,
I am ready for a quieter life now. But I can't rest while
a man like Moriarty is walking the streets of London.
When at last I win my fight against him, I will know that
I have finished my work as a detective.'

'But who is he?' I asked. 'What has he done?'

'He comes from an old English family, but crime is
in his blood. He is very clever, and was a professor in
his early twenties. But there were always many dark
stories about him, and ten years ago, he came to live in
London. You know, Watson, that no one understands
the criminal world of London as well as me. For years, I
have seen a strong hand at work in many of the crimes
that happen here. Again and again, I have tried to find
the evil genius behind them. At last, I learned who it
was – Moriarty, the great professor!

'He is a clever man, Watson, a real thinker,' Holmes
went on. 'He is at the centre of a very large organization
of dangerous criminals. He does nothing himself, but he
sits quietly there, making plans. Then he moves his men
carefully from one place to another – a burglary here,
a murder there. Sometimes the police catch the thief or
the murderer, but they never even hear of the professor –

he is too clever and too quick.

'I knew that I had to destroy his organization,' said Holmes. 'But the professor never leaves a clue. After three months, I still didn't have the necessary evidence. For the first time, I was fighting against someone who could plan things as well as me. Luckily, in the end, he made a small mistake – only a very small one – and I made my move. Now, at last, I have nearly caught him. I need to wait for three more days, and then by Monday, the police will have their evidence. We'll solve forty crimes, and some very evil men will go to prison. But we must be careful – escape is possible, even at the last minute.'

Holmes began to walk up and down the room. 'Of course,' he said, 'Professor Moriarty knew what I was doing all the time. He has tried to hide the evidence from me, and to stop me investigating. It has been the most terrible fight! But this morning, I made my last important move. Later, I was sitting in my room at Baker Street, thinking about the case, when the door opened and Moriarty himself walked in.'

Holmes was very excited now, and I said nothing more while he told me about his meeting with Professor Moriarty. This is what he said...

CHAPTER 2

Holmes's Story

My heart jumped a little when I saw Moriarty in the doorway. He is very tall and thin, and he has small eyes that sit deep in his white face. His head moves slowly from side to side when he looks at you, like a strange animal. I knew at once that my life was in danger, so I quickly took a small gun from my desk and put it in my dressing-gown pocket.

But Moriarty knew what I was doing. 'It's dangerous to keep a gun in your dressing-gown pocket,' he said.

'It's dangerous to keep a gun in your dressing-gown pocket.'

I took the gun out and put it, ready to use, on the table in front of me.

'You don't know who I am, I see,' he said. He was smiling, but when I looked at his eyes, I was pleased to have the gun there.

'No,' I said, 'I know very well who you are. Please sit down. I am free for five minutes if you have anything to say.'

'I do have something to say. But you already know what that is.'

'Then perhaps you already know my answer.'

'You are taking a dangerous road,' said Moriarty. 'Won't you turn back?'

'No,' I replied. 'What are you going to do about it?'

'You must drop this case against me, Mr Holmes,' he said, and his head moved slowly again from side to side when he looked at me. 'You really must, you know.'

'I'll drop it after Monday,' I said.

'No, no,' he replied. 'You're a clever man, and you know that there is only one way out. You must drop it now. I have greatly enjoyed working against you, Mr Holmes, and I'll be very sorry if I have to destroy you. You smile, sir, but I truly will be sorry.'

'There is always danger in my work,' I replied.

'This is not just danger,' he said. 'It is immediate death.'

I stood up. 'This has been a pleasant conversation, but

I have important business, I'm afraid.'

Moriarty also stood up, and looked at me.

'Well, well,' he said at last, 'I'm sorry for you. I've done what I could. I know what you're planning. But the police will never arrest me, and you will never win against me. If you try to destroy me, Mr Holmes, I'll destroy you first. You can be sure of that.'

'I will die happily at your hands, Mr Moriarty, if I can free the people of this country from you.'

'Only one of those things is going to happen!' he said angrily. 'You will never destroy *me*!' And he turned his back on me and left the room.

'You will never destroy me!'

CHAPTER 3

Fast Train to Dover

'So, Watson, that was my strange conversation with Professor Moriarty,' Holmes said. 'When he talks of destroying me, I know that he means it. His men have tried to kill me today.'

'What, already?' I cried.

'My dear Watson, Professor Moriarty moves fast. I was in Oxford Street at lunchtime, when suddenly a two-horse coach came quickly round the corner and drove at me. Luckily, I jumped onto the footpath, and was fine. Then, while I was walking down Vere Street, a rock fell from the top of a house and crashed at my feet. The police investigated, but they couldn't find anybody up there. I took a cab after that and spent the day at my brother's house in Pall Mall. But on my way here this evening, someone ran up to me and tried to hit me with a heavy stick, and I had to fight him off. The police have arrested him, but he won't tell them anything about Moriarty, I'm sure. This is why I had to close your shutters when I arrived here. And it's why I shall leave your house by the back door.'

'Won't you spend the night here?' I said, looking worriedly at Holmes.

'Moriarty's men have tried to kill me today.'

'No, my friend, it is too dangerous for you. On Monday, the police will make their arrests and everything will be fine. They don't need me here while they're doing that, so until then, I'm going to leave the country for a while. That's the best thing for me. Will you come? We must start tomorrow morning.'

'I'm not busy this week,' I said. 'So, yes, I will.'

'Good. Now listen carefully, Watson, because you and I are working against the cleverest man and the strongest criminal organization in Europe. Send your suitcase

to Victoria Station tonight. In the morning, ask your
servant to call a cab. Don't take the first or the second
one that arrives, but take the third. Drive to Lowther
Arcade, and then run through the building into the next
street. Be there by 9.15. There will be another cab there.
Get in, and the driver will take you to Victoria Station
to catch the fast train to Dover.'

'Where shall I meet you?'

'On the train. I'll reserve the carriage that's second
from the front.'

With a few more quick words, Holmes left the house
by the kitchen door, and climbed over the back garden
wall into the street.

The next day, I did what Holmes wanted. All went
well. My suitcase was waiting for me at the station, and
I found the right carriage. But Holmes was not there,
and I started to worry. I knew that he was in great
danger, and only seven minutes before our train needed
to leave, I still could not see him.

While I was waiting, and worrying, I helped an old
Italian man. He wanted his suitcase to stay on the train
until Paris, but he only spoke a little English. So I asked
someone at the station about it for him, and he thanked
me warmly. Then I looked around again for Holmes,
and at last sat down in our carriage.

I was surprised when I found the old Italian man in
the seat opposite me in the carriage. I knew that it was

I found the old Italian man in the seat opposite me.

a mistake because the carriage was for Holmes and me. But my Italian was worse than his English, so I said nothing, and looked worriedly out of the window. All the train doors were shut, when...

'My dear Watson,' said a voice, 'you haven't even said good morning to me.'

I turned, in great surprise. The empty eyes of the Italian man brightened, the thin mouth smiled, and the years fell away from his old face. He was changing into Holmes in front of my eyes!

'Holmes!' I cried. 'It's you!'

'I had to be careful,' he said softly. 'I think that they're following us. Ah yes! There's Moriarty himself.'

The train was already moving, and through the window, I saw a tall, thin man with an evil face. He was running through the crowds, shouting. But he could not stop the train, which was leaving the station already.

Holmes took off his old Italian hat and coat, and sat back with a laugh. Then he said, 'We must plan what we are going to do next.'

'But Holmes,' I said, 'everything is all right now. He has missed the train!'

'My dear Watson, this man is very clever, and he will stop at nothing. Our train waits for a while at Canterbury. Moriarty will pay for a special train, which will take him very fast to Dover, with no stops. He will catch us there, while we're waiting for the boat to France.'

'Why don't you ask the police to arrest him at Dover?' I said.

'If I do that, it will destroy three months' work. The police will catch Moriarty, but all the other criminals who work with him will escape. No, this is what we will do: we'll get out at Canterbury, travel by road to Newhaven, and take a boat from there to Belgium. Moriarty will wait for us in Dover, but he won't find us there.'

Soon after we left the train at Canterbury, Holmes put his hand on my arm. 'You see?' he said. 'Here he comes.'

Holmes was right; we could hear a train. We hid

behind some large suitcases, and waited while the special train went through the station with a great noise.

'This time, I have been cleverer than him,' said Holmes. 'So, Watson, the important question now is: shall we have an early lunch here, or eat when we get to Newhaven?'

We hid behind some large suitcases, and waited.

CHAPTER 4

In the Mountains

We travelled by boat from Newhaven to Belgium that night and spent two days there before we went on to France. On Monday morning, Holmes sent a telegram to the London police, and in the evening, a reply was waiting at our hotel. When Holmes opened it, he cried angrily, 'I knew it! He has escaped!'

'Moriarty?' I asked.

'Yes. They have arrested all the other criminals, but they did not get him. Watson, you must go back to England now.'

'Why?' I said.

'We're in great danger here. I've destroyed this man's organization, and his life's work. He will only rest when he has found me, and he'll follow me all over Europe. You must go home.'

But I could not agree. Holmes was my oldest and greatest friend, and I did not want to leave him. He tried to tell me how dangerous it was, but for once I said that I would not listen. So that night, we travelled on together.

From France, we went over the mountains into Switzerland. The countryside was beautiful, and all around us there were little villages, green fields, and snowy mountain-tops. It was a pleasant week. But

Holmes never forgot that we were in danger. He was always looking around, and every time we walked or drove past people, he watched them carefully. Once, I remember, a large rock crashed to the ground just behind us. Immediately, Holmes ran up the hill above us and looked around; he saw no one.

But he was enjoying our holiday together, I could see, and he talked happily to me while we walked. Again and again he said, 'You know, Watson, if I can free the world from Moriarty and his evil plans, I'll be happy to bring my work to an end. He is the most dangerous criminal in Europe, and when the police catch him, it will be the greatest day in my life as a detective.'

A large rock crashed to the ground just behind us.

On May 3rd, we arrived at the little village of Meiringen, and found a small hotel. The landlord spoke English well, and we asked him about a good walk for the next day. He told us to walk to Rosenlaui and to stop at the Reichenbach Falls, a famous waterfall about two hours from the hotel.

So on May 4th, Holmes and I started our walk, and after some time, we came to the Reichenbach Falls. It is a truly terrible place. A great green wall of water crashes noisily down the steep side of the mountain. Hundreds of yards below, it falls into a deep hole in the black rock. All the time, there are clouds of water-drops above the waterfall, like smoke from a burning house. Down there in its deep, deep hole, the river turns and moves like a mad thing.

We stood there and looked down at the water breaking on the black rocks. The strange sound of it came up from far below, like a wild shout.

There is a footpath to the waterfall, but it comes to an end after a few yards, and the traveller has to go back the same way. We were starting to go back when a boy ran up to us with a letter from our landlord.

'Listen to this, Holmes,' I said, reading the letter. 'An Englishwoman arrived at the hotel soon after we left. She's very ill, and wants an English doctor. Our landlord says that she's dying, and he asks me to hurry back and help her. What do you think, Holmes? I don't want to

We looked down at the water breaking on the black rocks.

leave you alone, but I can't really say no.'

'You needn't worry, Watson,' said Holmes. 'I'll stay here for a while and then walk slowly over the hill to Rosenlaui. You can meet me there this evening.'

And so, that was what we agreed. I turned away, with one last look at Holmes. He was standing with his back against the wall of rock, and he was looking down at the crash and fall of the water. His walking-stick was beside him.

When I got near the bottom of the hill, I looked back up. I could not see the waterfall, but I could see the footpath to it. A man was walking quickly along it. I could not see him clearly, and in my hurry, I soon forgot him.

I arrived at Meiringen about an hour later, and the landlord was at the door of the hotel.

'Well,' I said, 'she is no worse, I hope?'

A look of surprise came into his face, and my heart felt suddenly heavy.

'You didn't write this?' I cried, pulling the letter from my pocket. 'There is no dying Englishwoman in the hotel?'

'No, there isn't!' he replied. 'But that's the hotel writing-paper! Ah, the tall Englishman who arrived here after you left this morning – perhaps he wrote it...'

I did not wait to hear any more from the landlord. I was already running back up the village street to the waterfall, shaking all over, and terribly afraid.

CHAPTER 5

A Last Word

I went as fast as possible, but the footpath was very steep, and it took me more than an hour to get back to the Reichenbach Falls. I could not see Holmes anywhere, and when I shouted, only my voice came back from the mountains around me.

Then I saw Holmes's walking-stick. I felt cold inside. So he did not walk on to Rosenlaui. He stayed there on that narrow footpath, with a wall of rock on one side, and a steep drop on the other, and waited for his enemy. And who knows what terrible thing happened then?

I stood there for a minute or two. My head felt empty, and I could not think. Then I had an idea: I decided to work like Holmes, and examine the place carefully. I looked at the ground first. The footpath was wet, so I could easily see two people's footprints. They went away from me to the end of the footpath above the waterfall, and no footprints came back. On the ground at the end of the footpath, there was evidence of a fight – a fight to the death. I lay on my stomach and looked down into the deep black hole, full of crashing water. I shouted, but only that strange cry of the waterfall came to my ears.

But there was a last word from my friend. When I looked again at his walking-stick, I found a small square of paper under it. It was a page from Holmes's notebook, with my name on it. His writing was as strong and clear as usual. This is what the note said:

My dear Watson,

Mr Moriarty is kindly waiting while I write these few words to you. Then he and I will finish talking about the questions which lie between us. He has explained to me how he has stayed out of the hands of the English police, and how he found you and me here in Switzerland. I said that the man is a genius, and I was not wrong. The world will be free of him very soon, and I am happy to know that. Perhaps my friends, and you most of all, my dear Watson, will think that the cost is too high. But I can think of no better end to my work than this. I knew that there was no dying Englishwoman in Meiringen, I'm sorry to say. I knew that Moriarty was coming to find me.

Tell Inspector Patterson to look for all the evidence against Moriarty's organization in my desk, in a blue box. Everything which belongs to me will go to my brother. I spoke to him about this before I left England. Please say goodbye to your wife for me, and, my dear friend, I am

Very truly yours,

Sherlock Holmes

It was a page from Holmes's notebook.

This story is nearly at an end. Many people came to investigate the case and examine the footpath at the Reichenbach Falls. The two men were fighting, they said, when they fell to their deaths together – and we will never find their bodies. The world's most dangerous criminal and the world's greatest detective will lie for all time at the bottom of those terrible waters.

All the people in Moriarty's organization went to prison because of Holmes's evidence, but we did not learn any more about the professor. I do not think that anyone will cry for Moriarty, but I have lost a true friend – the best and cleverest man that I have ever known.

arrest *(n & v)* when the police take a person away to ask them questions about a crime

break in *(v)* to break the door or window of a place because you want to go in and steal something; **break-in** *(n)*

burglar *(n)* a person who goes into a building to steal things

burglary *(n)* the crime of stealing things from a building

cab *(n)* *(in the past)* a small coach that takes you from one place to another when you pay (like a taxi today)

carriage *(n)* one of the parts of a train where people sit

case *(n)* a crime for the police to investigate

clear *(adj)* easy to see, hear, or understand

clue *(n)* something that helps when you are trying to solve a crime

coach *(n)* *(in the past)* a vehicle (like a car, bus, etc.) with four wheels; horses pulled it

colonel *(n)* an important officer in the army

countryside *(n)* a place with fields, woods, farms, etc., that is away from big towns

destroy *(v)* to break or stop something

dressing-gown *(n)* You wear a dressing-gown in your home; it is like a big, soft coat.

Europe *(n)* a group of countries in the north of the world, including France, Germany, Spain, and Italy; **European** *(adj)*

evidence *(n)* things that you find or see, which help you to know that something is true

evil *(adj)* very, very bad and unkind

examine *(v)* to look carefully at something or somebody

footpath *(n)* a way across a piece of land; people can walk on it

footprint *(n)* a picture on the ground from your foot or shoe

genius *(n)* a very clever person

heart *(n)* the part of your body that pushes the blood around

hedge *(n)* a line of small trees around a garden or field

idea *(n)* a plan, or something you think of

investigate *(v)* to try to find out about something

land *(n)* a piece of ground

landlord *(n)* a person who takes money from other people because they are living or staying in his/her house or room

lawsuit *(n)* when people go to a court of law because they cannot agree about something

lie *(n)* something that is not true

mad *(adj)* ill in your head

organization *(n)* a group of people who work together

pleasant *(adj)* nice, enjoyable, or friendly

professor *(n)* a university teacher

reserve *(v)* to ask a restaurant, hotel, train office, etc. to keep a table, room, or seat for you at a later time

reward *(n)* You give a reward to somebody because they help you or do something good.

rock *(n)* the stone that is in the ground and in mountains

servant *(n)* a person who works in another person's house, doing work like cooking and cleaning

shutters *(n)* Shutters are like small doors that go across a window, to shut out the light.

sir *(n)* a name for an important man

solve *(v)* to find the answer to a question

steep *(adj)* when something, e.g. a hill or a road, goes up quickly from a low place to a high place

telegram *(n)* *(in the past)* a short note from one person to another, which could arrive more quickly than a letter

torn *(adj)* Clothes, paper, etc. are torn when you break them in two or more pieces, or make a hole in them.

yard *(n)* nearly a metre

Living in Holmes's London

At the time of the early Sherlock Holmes stories, in the 1890s, London was getting bigger and bigger. People were moving to towns and cities like London to look for work. But the pay was not good, and not everyone could find a job, so many people were very poor. They lived in small, dirty rooms, and often became ill and died young. Many families had to send their children out to work, too. But there were a small number of people who had good jobs or who did not need to work because they had money from their family. They lived very comfortably, like Sherlock Holmes and Dr Watson.

Travel

When Holmes wanted to escape from Moriarty, he reserved a carriage on the fast train from London to Dover. Train travel was very cheap in Sherlock Holmes's day, and many people travelled around Britain this way. You could even pay for a 'special' train, like Moriarty, and travel alone in it.

In London there were buses, coaches, trams, and cabs, and horses pulled these. London needed fifty thousand horses to get people from one place to another in the 1890s. People also used boats to travel across London.

The Postal Service

By 1880, postmen brought letters to people's homes and businesses in London up to twelve times a day. On Sundays there was no post. When someone posted a letter in London at 8.45 a.m., it usually arrived at a London address at about 10 a.m. on the same day. People could also send telegrams, which arrived even faster than letters.

The post was very good in other places in Britain, too. A letter that left central London at 8 p.m. usually arrived at any of the larger towns in England or Scotland the next morning.

READ & RESEARCH Are these statements true or false? Do some research to find the answers.

1 In 1801, around one million people lived in London, but by 1899, there were more than 6.5 million.

2 The London bus company spent £20,000 a year on horseshoes in the 1890s.

3 The British Post Office delivered 1,700,000 letters to homes and offices in 1890.

city *(n)* a big and important town
tram *(n)* a bus that moves along tracks (called rails) in the road

Think Ahead

1 Read the back cover of the book. Choose one answer.

1 In these stories, Holmes investigates two crimes in London.

2 Nobody dies in these stories.

3 Holmes's friend is Doctor Watson, and his enemy is Professor Moriarty.

2 How much do you know about Sherlock Holmes? Tick (✓) one box for each sentence.

	YES	NO	DON'T KNOW
1 He is married.	☐	☐	☐
2 He lives in Baker Street, London.	☐	☐	☐
3 He has a good friend called Watson.	☐	☐	☐
4 He enjoys going on holiday.	☐	☐	☐
5 He works very hard on his cases.	☐	☐	☐

3 RESEARCH Find out the answers to these questions about Sir Arthur Conan Doyle.

1 When was he born?

2 What was his job before he became a famous writer?

3 How many Sherlock Holmes stories did he write?

4 When did he die?

Chapter Check

The Dead Coachman

CHAPTER 1 Correct the underlined words.

1 Holmes sent Watson a <u>letter</u> from France.

2 There was a <u>murder</u> at Mr Acton's house.

3 At the colonel's house, the servant came with news of a <u>burglary</u>.

4 William was the Cunninghams' <u>gardener</u>.

5 Acton and Cunningham had the <u>smallest</u> houses in the village.

CHAPTER 2 Complete the sentences with the names of people in the story.

Alec   Dr Watson   Inspector Forrester   Mr Cunningham
Sherlock Holmes   William Kirwan

1 _____ came to visit Sherlock Holmes at breakfast-time.

2 _____ was hoping to keep Holmes away from the case.

3 At the time of the shooting, _____ was in bed.

4 When _____ heard a noise, he ran downstairs.

5 _____ was fighting with another man.

6 _____ wanted everyone to go to the Cunninghams' house together.

CHAPTER 3 Are these sentences true or false?

1 William's mother was very helpful to the police.
2 There were footprints on the ground outside the Cunninghams' back door.
3 The inspector did not tell the Cunninghams about the note in William's hand.
4 Mr Cunningham wrote 'one' on Holmes's paper.
5 Mr Cunningham was happy to give a reward.

CHAPTER 4 Match the sentences with the people who say them in the story. Who is each person speaking to?

Alec   Inspector Forrester
Mr Cunningham   Sherlock Holmes

1 'Have you seen everything now?'
2 'Look what you've done!'
3 'Wait here, all of you! That man is mad!'
4 'Drop it!'

CHAPTER 5 Tick (✓) the three sentences which are true.

1 The Cunninghams broke into Mr Acton's house.
2 Mr Acton saw the Cunninghams at his house, and asked for money to keep quiet.
3 Alec and his father wrote a letter and sent it to William.
4 William came to the Cunninghams' house at lunchtime.
5 Alec had the rest of William's note.

The Last Mystery

CHAPTER 1 Answer the questions about people in the story.

Who...

1 moved away from Baker Street?

2 was away on a family visit?

3 was in danger?

4 was 'the world's greatest criminal'?

CHAPTER 2 Match the sentence halves to make a conversation between Holmes and Moriarty.

1 I've done...

2 I am free for five minutes...

3 You know that...

4 I'll be very sorry...

5 It's dangerous...

6 I know what...

a you're planning.

b there is only one way out.

c if you have anything to say.

d what I could.

e to keep a gun in your dressing-gown pocket.

f if I have to destroy you.

CHAPTER 3 Choose the correct words to complete the sentences.

1 Holmes said that Moriarty moves *slowly* / *fast*.

2 A man with a *gun* / *stick* tried to kill Holmes.

3 There was an old *Italian* / *French* man on the train.

4 Moriarty *caught* / *missed* Holmes at Victoria Station.

5 Holmes and Watson hid behind *a train* / *some suitcases*.

CHAPTER 4 Complete the sentences with the place names below.

Belgium   Meiringen   Reichenbach   Rosenlaui

Holmes and Watson…

1 spent two days in _____.

2 arrived at the village of _____ on May 3rd.

3 went to visit the _____ Falls on May 4th.

4 planned to spend the evening of May 4th at
_____.

CHAPTER 5 Tick (✓) the three sentences which are true.

1 When Watson saw the footprints, he knew that Holmes was alive.

2 Moriarty did not know that Holmes wrote a note.

3 Moriarty and Holmes had a fight.

4 When he wrote the note, Holmes knew that he was going to die.

5 Holmes destroyed Moriarty's criminal organization.

Focus on Vocabulary

1 Complete the sentences with the correct words.

arrest   dressing-gown   investigate
organization   reserve   shutters

1 People often asked Holmes to _____ difficult
   cases.

2 Alec put the note in the pocket of his _____.

3 Holmes asked the inspector to _____ the
   Cunninghams and take them to the police station.

4 Holmes closed the window _____ in Watson's
   room.

5 Holmes decided to _____ a carriage on the
   fast train.

6 Everyone in Moriarty's _____ went to prison in
   the end.

2 Replace the underlined words with the words below.

footpath   genius   pleasant   servant   solves

1 The colonel had a <u>man who did things for him around
   the house</u>.

2 Moriarty was a <u>very clever man</u>.

3 Holmes and Watson spent a very <u>nice</u> week in
   Switzerland.

4 There was a <u>way for walkers</u> to the Reichenbach Falls.

5 Holmes always <u>finds the answers to</u> his cases.

Focus on Language

1 **Complete the sentences with *who*, *which*, or *what*.**

That's the man _____ stole the money.
That's the man who stole the money.

1 I'll explain _____ you have to do.

2 I saw an old man _____ was selling newspapers.

3 The police didn't know _____ happened next.

4 He put his hand on the gun, _____ was on the table.

5 The girl _____ wrote that letter isn't here today.

6 We got on the train, _____ didn't leave for a long time.

2 **DECODE** **Read the text from the story and underline the words *this* and *that*.**

Holmes put his foot quietly on the gun. 'Keep that,' he said to the inspector. 'They used it to kill William, I'm sure. But this is what we really wanted.' He held up a piece of paper.

3 **Match the examples of *this* and *that* above with the meanings below.**

1 a piece of paper

2 the gun

4 **Where is each of these things?**

Discussion

1 **THINK CRITICALLY** Read the conversation below. Who do you agree with most, A or B?

A: In my opinion, Watson was wrong to leave Holmes alone at the Reichenbach Falls.

B: That's not fair. If Holmes knew that there was no dying Englishwoman, why didn't he tell Watson? I think that Holmes wanted to die like that.

A: I don't agree. My view is that Holmes died because of Watson's mistake.

B: No way! Poor Watson!

2 Complete the phrases from the conversation in exercise 1 for giving your opinion or disagreeing. Then write O or D.

1 In my _____, ...

2 That's not _____.

3 I _____ that...

4 I don't _____.

5 My _____ is...

6 No _____!

3 **COMMUNICATE** Discuss the statement below with a partner. Use the phrases in exercise 2 and your own ideas.

Detective stories are more interesting than romances.

Sir Arthur Conan Doyle wrote sixty stories about Sherlock Holmes, and people around the world love these mysteries. But Sherlock Holmes is not the only famous detective from books.

HERCULE POIROT
From: Belgium
Appears in: The stories of Agatha Christie
Detective methods: He is very interested in how criminals think and feel. People like talking to him, and he can often find out what he wants to know from them.
More about him: He is always very tidily dressed and he often wears a hat. He hates it when his clothes or shoes get dirty.
Works with: A friend called Captain Hastings (in some of the stories), who helps him solve crimes.
Famous case: 'Murder on the Orient Express'

D.B. RUSSELL
From: USA
Appears in: *CSI: Crime Scene Investigation*
Detective methods: He is very clever, and knows a lot about flowers and gardens. When he visits a place to investigate a crime, he examines all the clues very carefully.
More about him: When he was a child, he moved from place to place with his mother and father, who made money from playing music.
Works with: Julie Finlay

MISS JANE MARPLE
From: England
Appears in: The stories of Agatha Christie
Detective methods: She is not a detective, just an old lady who lives a quiet life – but she is very clever. She can solve difficult crimes because she remembers cases like them in her village from many years before.
More about her: She lives in a beautiful village in the English countryside.
Works with: Sir Henry Clithering (in some of the stories), who was once a policeman, and can often give her useful clues.
Famous case: 'The Body in the Library'

1 **Read the profiles. Who...**

   1 can remember things from a long time ago?

   2 likes to look inside a criminal's head?

   3 travelled around a lot in early life?

2 **Match the photos with the profiles.**

3 **CREATE** Now find out more information about Sherlock Holmes or another famous detective and write a profile for him/her like the ones above.

Sir Arthur Conan Doyle was born in Edinburgh, Scotland, in 1859. His mother loved books and told him wonderful stories when he was a boy. He left home to go to school in England when he was nine years old. He was very unhappy there, but he was good at sport, and, like his mother, could tell stories very well, so the younger boys sat and listened to him for hours.

After school, Conan Doyle studied to be a doctor at Edinburgh University. Conan Doyle's teacher at university, Dr Joseph Bell, was a very clever man who watched and studied everything very carefully. It was Dr Bell who gave Conan Doyle his ideas for Sherlock Holmes.

While Conan Doyle was studying, he wrote two short stories, and began to make a little money from his writing. After he left university, Conan Doyle worked as a doctor and as a writer, too. He married Louisa Hawkins in 1885, and in 1886 he began writing *A Study in Scarlet*. This was his first novel about the detective Sherlock Holmes – a strange genius who lives at 221B Baker Street in London. Holmes can find the answer to any problem and often explains how easy it is to his slow-thinking friend Dr Watson.

Readers began to be very interested in Sherlock Holmes when *The Sign of Four* was published in 1890, and soon he was very famous. In 1891, Conan Doyle was very ill, and after this he stopped working as a doctor.

Conan Doyle liked writing novels about history like *The White Company* (1891), and he was soon bored with Sherlock Holmes. So, in *The Final Problem* (1893) (called *The Last Mystery* in this Bookworm story) he 'killed' him when Holmes and his famous enemy Professor Moriarty fell to their deaths at the Reichenbach Falls. But because people wanted more stories about Holmes, Conan Doyle had to bring him back to life in *The Hound of the Baskervilles* (1902) and many more stories.

Conan Doyle's first wife died in 1906, and in 1907 he married Jean Leckie, and moved to a large house in the English countryside. He already had two children, and he and Jean Leckie had three more. Conan Doyle wrote some plays at this time, and *The Lost World*, a science fiction novel. More Sherlock Holmes stories followed, too.

Conan Doyle also wanted to do public service: to work for his country. During the Second World War, he wrote many times to the War Office with clever ideas to help the British army. Conan Doyle also liked to investigate things himself, and he fought for people who were in prison for crimes that they did not do. He died in July 1930 at his home in Sussex.

If you liked this Bookworm, why not try...

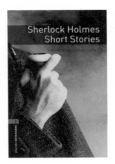

Sherlock Holmes Short Stories

STAGE 2

Sir Arthur Conan Doyle

Sherlock Holmes is the greatest detective of them all. He listens, and watches, and thinks. He listens to the steps coming up the stairs; he watches the door opening – and he knows what question the stranger will ask.

In these three short stories, Holmes has three visitors to the famous flat in Baker Street – visitors who bring their troubles to the only man in the world who can help them.

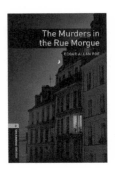

The Murders in the Rue Morgue

STAGE 2

Edgar Allan Poe

The room was on the fourth floor, and the door was locked – with the key on the inside. The windows were closed and fastened – on the inside. So how did the murderer escape? And whose were the two angry voices heard by the neighbours as they ran up the stairs? Nobody in Paris could find any answers to this mystery. Except Auguste Dupin, who could see more clearly than other people. The answers to the mystery were all there, but only a clever person could see them.